a slug in a salad is rather a fright;
a fly in your tea is a miserable sight;
but one of the things that I utterly hate
is finding a hare on the side of my plate.

a collection of the most
POINTLESS VERSES
of
SIMON DREW

Drawings and Verses
by Simon Drew

Cedric
was always
on his mobile fawn

ANTIQUE COLLECTORS' CLUB

to Caroline

a problem shared is gossip

©2006 Simon Drew
World copyright reserved

ISBN10: 1-905377-07-X
ISBN13: 978-1-905377-07-7

British Library Cataloguing-in-Publication Data
A catalogue record for this book is available from the British Library

Printed and bound in China
for the Antique Collectors' Club Ltd., Woodbridge, Suffolk

the wily gannet sits on granite
thus avoiding germs
and so this bird must feed on fish
for granite has no worms.

No movement comes from goose or cow or sheep
and farmyard sounds are muffled by the rain,
and when you think that everyone's asleep
the Bantam of the Opera sings again.

THE IMMACULATE CONFECTION

They chop up apples every day
They peel and pip and core them
There's Jill and Joy from Maidenhead,
This work will never bore them.

They chop up apples every day:
there's Norah, Sue and Brenda
and as they toil they chant and pray
for Christ's on their agenda.

They chop up apples every day
the pastry factory beavers
and while they cook their pies and cakes
they're God's dessert believers.

They chop up apples every day;
these Jills and Joys and Norahs.
And all the time they're singing hymns:
the Hallelujah corers.

SUPERSTITION

The wind was blowing cold
like a snort from an eskimo's nose.
The owl was hooting loud
in the day (which is odd, I suppose).
The chap with ice cream treats
was a man with a mission to sell
but how could anyone buy
from a man with no stories to tell?

Somewhere something moved:
how could that noise have occurred?
Was it a flapping bat
or the squawk from a colourful bird?
Or was it a croaking frog
or a whispering chatter of bears?
No: you must listen hard:
it was superdog saying his prayers.

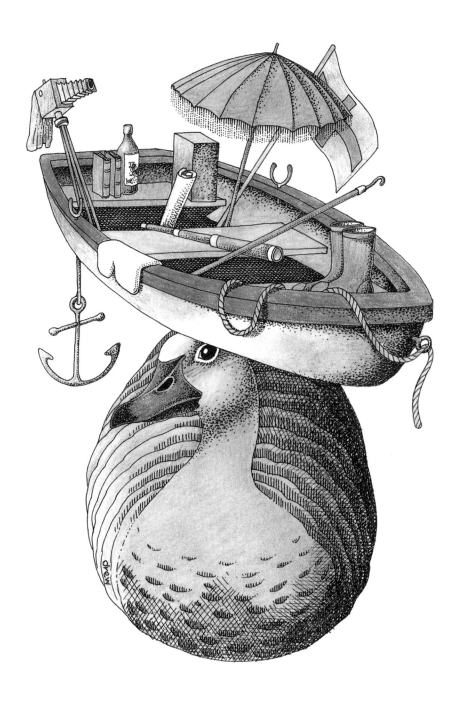

Needed on Voyage

Corkscrew, compass, anchor, sails,
thing to fire harpoon in whales,
boathook, biscuits, painters, rum,
thing to keep the sun off mum,
water, whisky, ice-cold beer,
thing to see when land is near,
rubber wellies, waterproofs,
thing to get the stones from hoofs,
starcharts, seacharts, satellite dish,
book to find the names of fish,
swimsuit, camera, dried food, flag:
put them all in one big bag.
Once you think you've got them all,
never leave the harbour wall.

A french philosophical feline
supported a sink full of jam.
This strange aberration
had one explanation:
"I sink and so therefore I am."

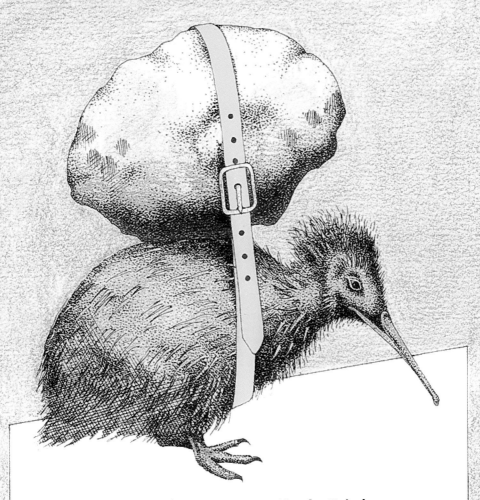

a flightless bird called Faith
began to carry boulders:
for years she took these weights
strapped between her shoulders;
and as you might expect
the sweat poured like a fountain,
but only time will tell
if Faith can move a mountain.

While walking through some farmyard pens
past ploughs with rusty blades,

14

amongst the turkeys, geese and hens,
he found the three of spades.

ONE PRISONER TO ANOTHER

① How will we escape this board ?
  Fight up every rung ?
  To find an anaconda's scored:
    we're wrenched from where we clung.

And every time we think we're floored
we feel like we've been stung,
but climb back up for our reward:
a python's flicking tongue.

② And here's another game we play
   with pawns and knights and kings
   always getting in our way
   when we want better things.

So will this chess game ever end?
The board's become a wreck.
Is your plumage tweed, my friend?
Or would you call it check,(mate)?

the moon was wrapped in mist
like the clingfilm round a pear
and the hills were growing darker
and the milkman wasn't there.

a friend of mine's a critic who's changed into a gull,
and though his life is brighter, his writing now seems dull;
for while his methods altered, he never lost his flair:
what he did on paper, he now does from the air.

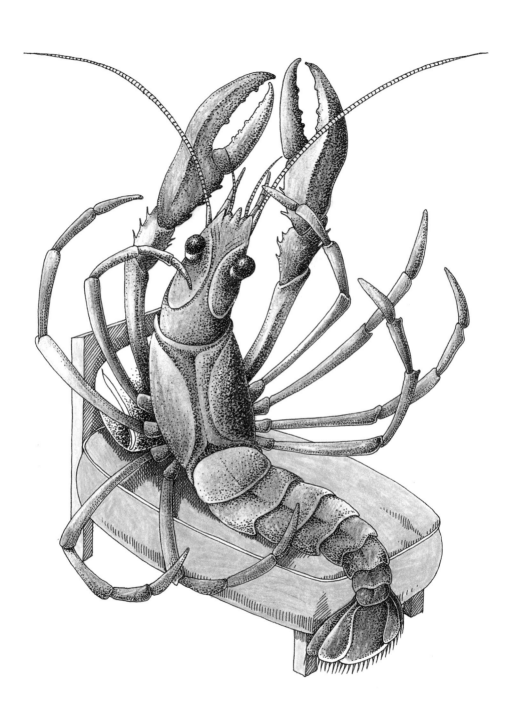

THE SEA BED

If a lobster can lie on a seabed
where are the sea pillows kept?
And if it is here in the daytime
where in the world has it slept?
If a willow can weep over water
how will we know if it's wept?
If a creeper can live on the willow
do we say, when it grows, it has crept?
If broom covers hillsides with yellow
how will they ever get swept?
If a frog can play leap-frog with no-one
how do we know when it's leapt?

a short story
in five
parts

THE HUNTER

1.

I once met a pig in a sweat in a sauna,
    a shy and a secretive beast;
he lives in a house called hide-pork corner
    "somewhere" he said "to the east."
(He uses the sauna to keep himself pink
for pigs are more vain than a person
                    might think.)

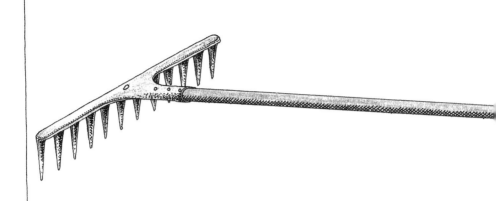

2

Life's pack of cards has been given a shuffle
   and dealt him a curious hand:
he has an ambition to hunt a great truffle,
   the greatest they'll find in the land.
He has no desire to seek second best;
this, he decrees, is the ultimate test.

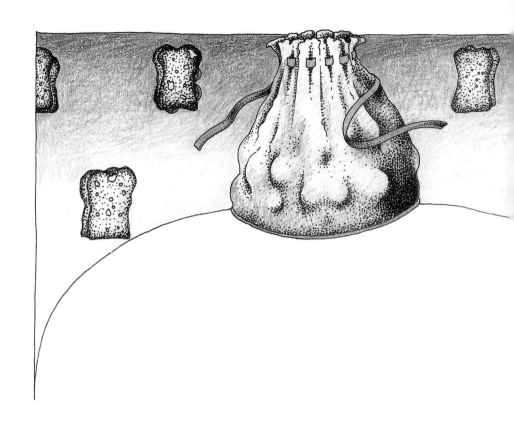

3

On Sundays he goes on his weekly
                            adventure,
  his sandwiches bursting with cheese
(for though this gives trouble with bits in
                            his denture
  the smell drives away all his fleas).
He carries a bag in a secretive way,
a bag that is heavy and canvas and grey.

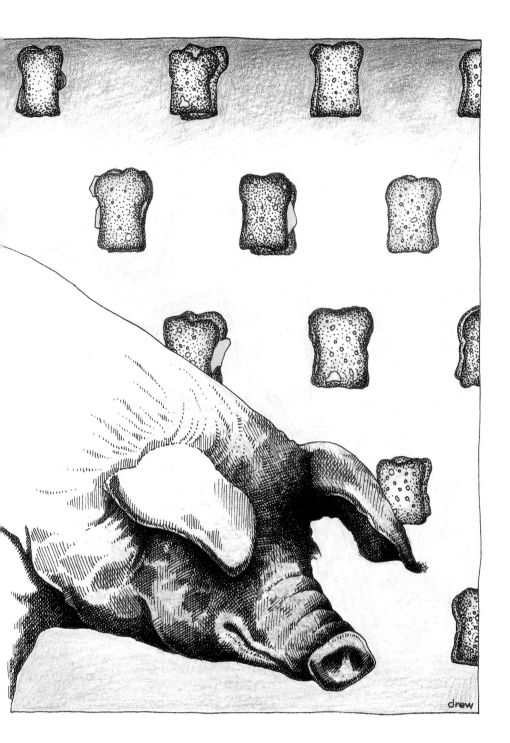

drew

29

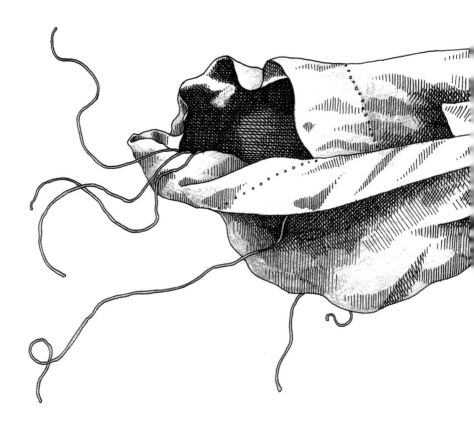

4

His nose is so large it's a problem to measure
"That organ's immense", you'll declare.
It picks up the scent of the underground treasure
with hardly a trace in the air.
This special proboscis is kept at its best
by keeping it wrapped in a light woollen vest.

drew

31

5

And when he's made sure of a truffle's
                          location
  He marks out the spot with some chalk;
This fine fungal growth is a dish's foundation
  (although he can't eat it with pork).
He uses a shovel to dig a great pit
and calls it a tool in his best earther kit.

drew

Last christmas Papa bought a reindeer,
to pull our toboggan, he said.
But it rained for the whole of december
so it played the piano instead.

A NEW BREED

I had a dream that I would soon fulfill,
to breed a dog that answered to my will.
I needed genes from bloodlines clean and pure,
untainted strains of which I could be sure.
And all my best endeavours soon bore fruit:
a tiny puppy – bright and soft and cute.

O come O come Emmanuel
For I've just bred a King Charles Spaniel.

BREAKFAST, PART ONE

On Tuesday last, without a sound
I'd woken, dressed and gone downstairs
expecting breakfast, but I found
a sight that took me unawares.

The sugar bowl showed signs of feet,
the butter's state you'd call distressed,
the marmalade was far from neat,
and someone had consumed the rest.

BREAKFAST, PART TWO

Today I rose and dressed in haste,
brought in the milk and fetched the post.
I tucked my shirt tails in my waist
and dreamed of scrambled egg on toast.

38

I found there'd been another raid:
(I caught a glimpse of running legs).
The table had been neatly laid
and so had half a dozen eggs.

A cherry's a berry to eat on its own.
In the soft centre you'll find there's a stone,
once it's removed you must eat the flesh whole
for these are the fruits of which life is a bowl.

Lenny's Drawer

Mrs da Vinci was always annoyed
Lenny, her son, would confess
that though he had faults he tried to avoid,
his bedroom was always a mess.

"Look at this drawer; it's a crying disgrace;
rubbish from goodness knows when.
And how did you get all that paint on
                                        your face?
Has Lisa been playing again?

You dream up contraptions like
                          submarine toys,
but never a knife to cut bread.
Why can't you be like the other young boys?
Invent something useful instead."

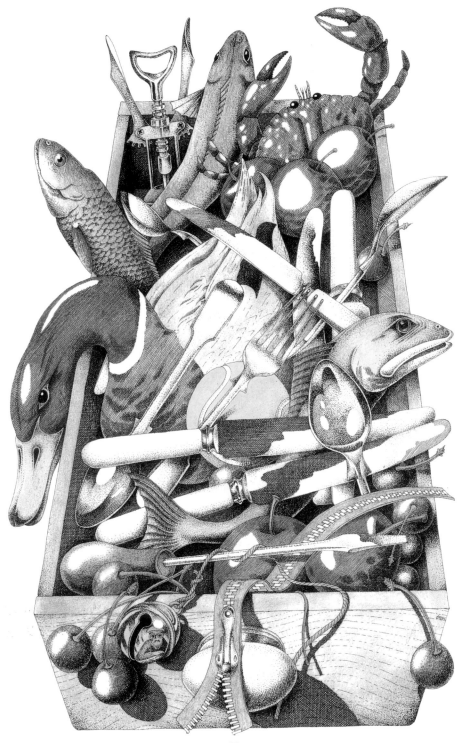

43

All around us dangers wait,
worse than any thriller:
somewhere hidden in a field
there lurks a cereal killer.

45

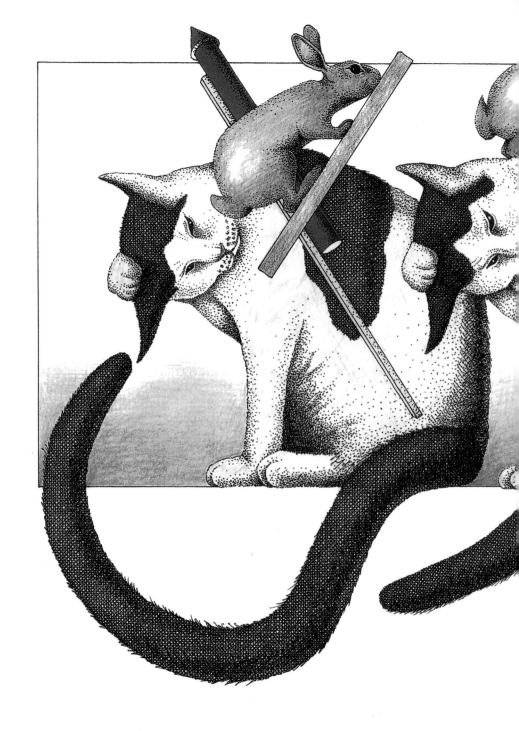

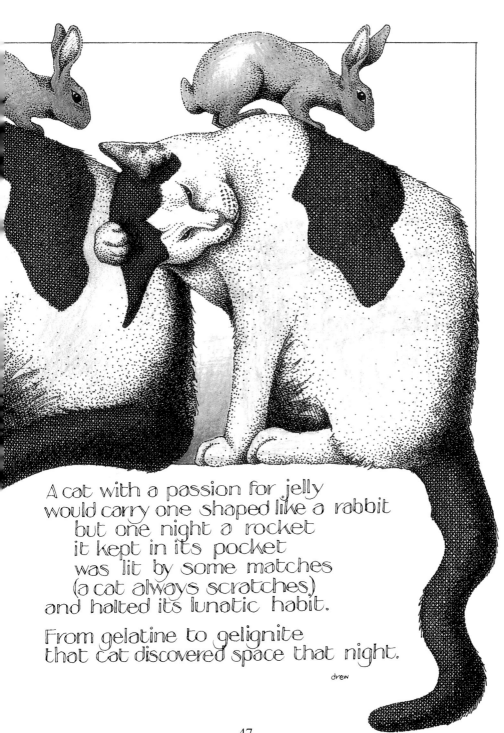

A cat with a passion for jelly
would carry one shaped like a rabbit
but one night a rocket
it kept in its pocket
was lit by some matches
(a cat always scratches)
and halted its lunatic habit.

From gelatine to gelignite
that cat discovered space that night.

drew

47

Ode to J.M.W. Turner

Turner was a hooligan,
a fact that's little known:
he drank too much on Friday nights
and wore a traffic cone.

His watercolours throbbed with life;
his vivid sunsets burst.
But every week on Friday nights
he thought of lager first.

He painted ships on weekdays
or gentle waterfalls
but when it came to Friday nights
he wrote on toilet walls.